curious about?

CHAPTER THREE

3

Bringing Home the Win

PAGE
16

Curious About is published by
Amicus Learning, an imprint of Amicus
P.O. Box 227, Mankato, MN 56002
www.amicuspublishing.us

Editors: Ana Brauer and Megan Siewert
Series Designer: Kathleen Petelinsek
Book Designer and Photo Researcher: Emily Dietz

Library of Congress Cataloging-in-Publication Data
Names: Koestler-Grack, Rachel A., 1973– author.
Title: Curious about breakaway roping / by Rachel Grack.
Description: Mankato, MN : Curious About is published by Amicus
Learning, [2025] | Series: Curious about Rodeo | Includes
bibliographical references and index. | Audience: Ages 6–9
years | Audience: Grades 2–3 | Summary: "Learn how cowboys
and cowgirls (and their horses) compete in breakaway roping
rodeo events in this question-and-answer book for elementary-
aged readers. Includes infographics and back matter to support
research skills along with table of contents, glossary, books and
websites for further research, and index"—Provided by publisher.
Identifiers: LCCN 2024015031 (print) | LCCN
2024015032 (ebook) | ISBN 9798892000857
(lib bdg) | ISBN 9798892001434 (paperback)
| ISBN 9798892002011 (ebook)
Subjects: LCSH: Calf roping—Juvenile literature.
Classification: LCC GV1834.45.C34 K644
2025 (print) | LCC GV1834.45.C34
(ebook) | DDC 791.8/4—dc23/eng/20240508
LC record available at https://lccn.loc.gov/2024015031
LC ebook record available at https://lccn.loc.gov/2024015032

Photo Credits: Alamy Stock Photo/Chris Aschenbrener,
2, 6, Jim Parkin, 18, Michelle Gilders, 3, 20–21, Sindre
Ellingsen, 17, Xinhua, 9; Associated Press/Jimmy May, 15;
Dreamstime/Michael Turner, 2, 10, 13, 5, 16; Getty Images/
AustralianLight, 14, FOTOGRAFIA INC., 7, RichLegg, 8,
Robert Alexander, 11; Shutterstock/Diane Garcia,
1; The Noun Project/1art, 19 (*top*), Adrien Coquet, 19
(*second from bottom*), Amethyst Studio, 19 (*second from top*),
Eucalyp, 22–23 (*lasso*), izzul fikry, 19 (*bottom*), OURSEL
Alexandre, 19 (*middle*), Steve Laing, 22–23 (*saddle*)

Printed in China

What is breakaway roping?

It is a rodeo sport. **Contestants** on horseback rope a calf. The chute opens. A calf runs into the arena. The roper blasts out of the box, throws the rope, and makes a catch. The rope "breaks away" from the **saddle horn**. *Time!*

At pro rodeos, contestants perform roping and riding skills for a chance to win a money prize.

FAST CATCH

Breakaway roping is a
women's sport in the rodeo.

Who can do it?

Breakaway roping is a women's event at professional rodeos. But both boys and girls can compete at youth rodeos. Kids can enter breakaway events at age nine. But they start riding and roping much younger. Roping on horseback takes lots of practice. Having a good horse helps.

Do the horses have special training?

Yes. Horses are so well trained they perform without commands. They know when to take off by the way the roper moves. They stop as soon as she throws. Many ropers use American Quarter Horses. They are smart and easy to train. Plus, they have the speed and strength needed for split-second roping.

FAST CATCH

DID
YOU KNOW?
American Quarter Horses
can make sudden stops.
The quicker the stop, the
faster the rope will break.

CHAPTER TWO

2

Why does the rider start behind a rope?

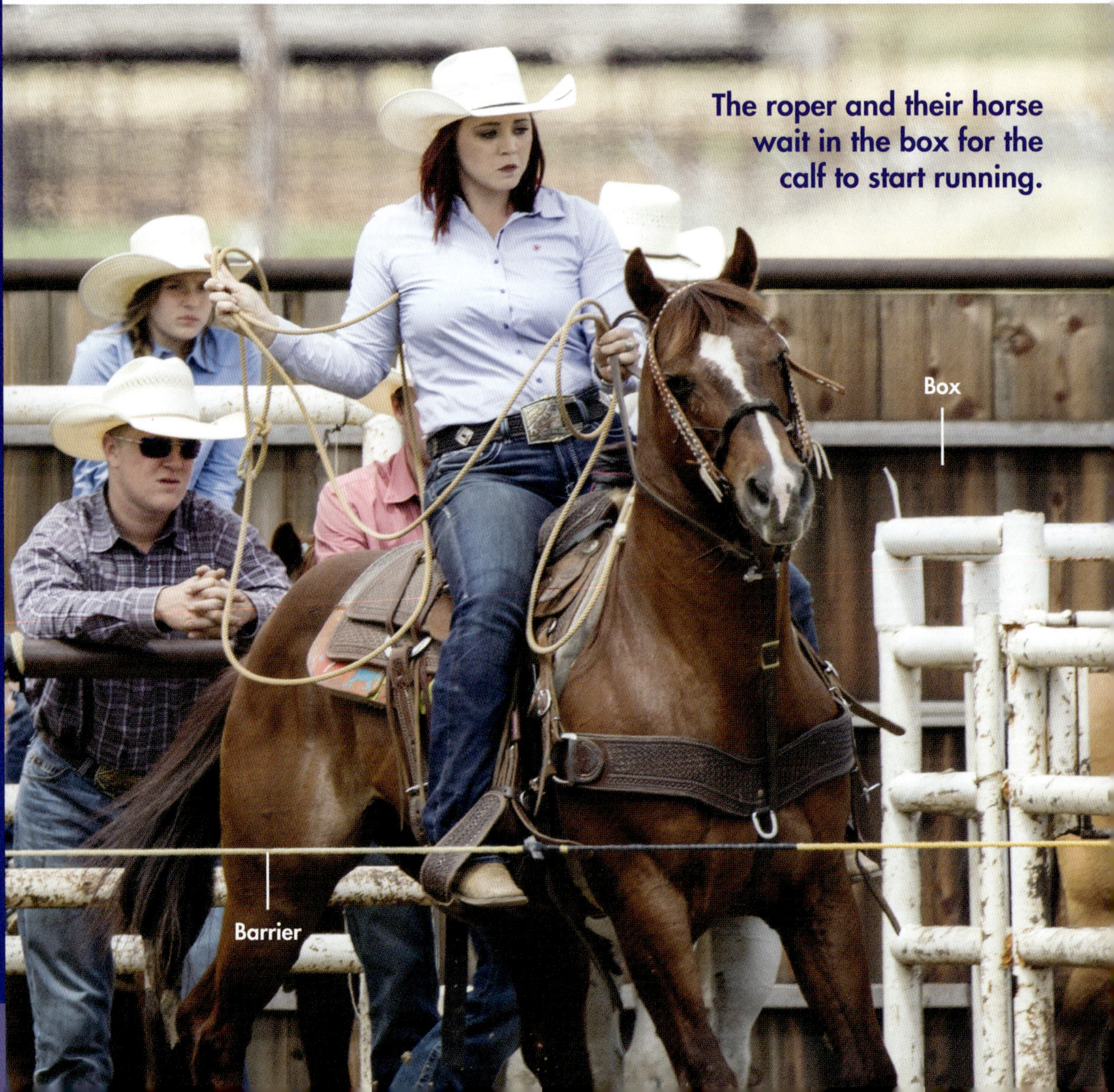

The roper and their horse wait in the box for the calf to start running.

That's the barrier. The rider must stay behind it until the calf gets a head start. A rope is tied around the calf's neck. It breaks loose when the calf reaches a certain distance. This causes the barrier rope to drop. The clock starts and the chase begins!

When does the rider rope the calf?

As fast as possible! She has one shot to make a **bell collar catch**. She aims for the calf's head. She swings and throws. It's a clean catch around the neck! The horse skids to a stop. The rope pulls tight. *Snap!*

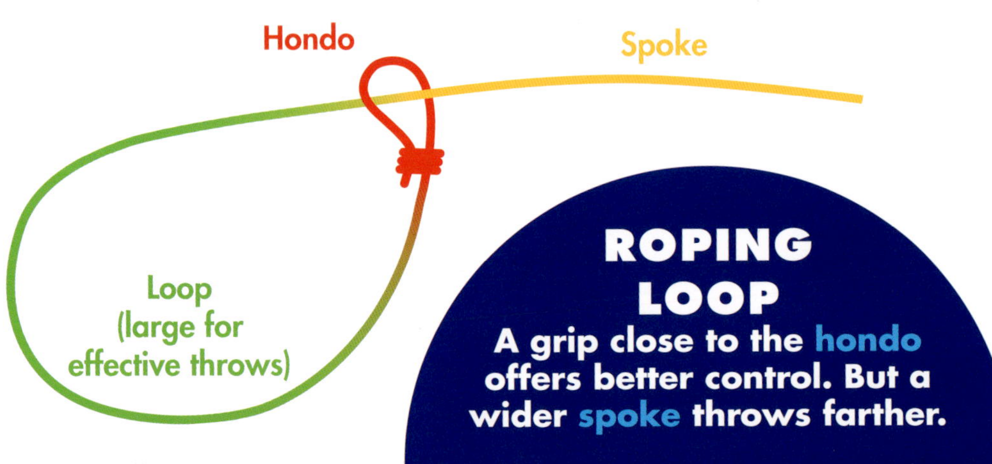

The bell collar catch is
the only catch allowed
in breakaway roping.

Why does the rope break?

The rope doesn't really break. It's a string around the saddle horn. Ropers tie a thin string to the rope, then tie it to the saddle horn. The sudden jerk from the calf snaps the string. The rope drops to the dirt. The clock stops.

Ropers tie a colorful string and a flag to the end of their rope. The colors help the judges see the rope better.

How do judges time ropers?

Breakaway roping is a quick event. Runs usually only last about 2–3 seconds.

The fastest time wins. But runs are hundredths of a
second apart. Judges must clock the exact time the
rope breaks. Ropers tie flags to the breakaway rope.
They are easier to see drop. Judges know just when
to stop the clock. *One*, *two*, and *time*!

Judges time the
ropers carefully
to know who has
the fastest time.

She broke the barrier. What does that mean?

Judges wave a flag when a rider is disqualified. A no score is also called "flagged out."

Oh no! Her horse left the box too soon. That tacks on a 10-second **penalty**. Ouch! Sometimes ropers get a "no score." She broke a different rule. Maybe she failed to make a fair catch. Out of the money this go-round!

ROPER THREW THE ROPE BEFORE CROSSING THE BARRIER

1

ROPER DID NOT LET GO OF THE ROPE

2

ROPER DID NOT MAKE A FAIR CATCH

3

ROPER TOUCHES THE ROPE AFTER THE CATCH

4

ROPER TAKES LONGER THAN 30 SECONDS TO MAKE A CATCH

5

Did she win?

Her horse did not break the barrier. She lets go of the rope. It was a bell collar catch! No other body parts got caught. She kept her hands off of the rope. And she finished with the fastest roping time. She wins a buckle. Yee-haw!

As of 2024, the world record for breakaway roping is 1.43 seconds.

ASK MORE QUESTIONS

How old do you have to be to rope?

Is roping hard to learn?

Try a BIG QUESTION: Could I be a roper?

SEARCH FOR ANSWERS

Search the library catalog or the Internet.
A librarian, teacher, or parent can help you.

Using Keywords
Find the looking glass.

Keywords are the most important words in your question.

If you want to know about:

- what age you can start roping, type: ABOUT YOUTH ROPING
- how to rope, type: ROPING SKILLS

FIND GOOD SOURCES

Here are some good, safe sources you can use in your research.
Your librarian can help you find more.

Books

Tie-Down Roping
by Rachel Grack, 2025.

Calf Roping
by Rochelle Groskreutz, 2021.

Internet Sites

Britannica Kids: Rodeos
https://kids.britannica.com/students/article/rodeo/276762
Britannica is an encyclopedia with educational information on many topics. Learn more about rodeos.

Kiddle: Calf Roping Facts for Kids
https://kids.kiddle.co/Calf_roping
Kiddle is an online encyclopedia for kids. Search for information on a wide variety of educational topics.

Every effort has been made to ensure that these websites are appropriate for children. However, because of the nature of the Internet, it is impossible to guarantee that these sites will remain active indefinitely or that their contents will not be altered.

SHARE AND TAKE ACTION

Watch breakaway roping.
Ask an adult to help you find videos of breakaway roping events.

Try roping a bale.
Get a lightweight lasso and give it a throw!

Take horseback riding classes.
Ropers are highly skilled on horseback. Learn to ride first!

Attend a rodeo.
Experience breakaway roping firsthand!

GLOSSARY

bell collar catch A loop landing around a calf's neck only; the only catch that will earn points.

contestants People who compete against each other in a sporting event.

hondo The loop knot tied on a lasso.

penalty A mark that counts against a score.

saddle horn The tall handgrip on a saddle.

spoke The distance between the hondo and your hand.

INDEX

About the Author

Rachel Grack has been writing children's nonfiction for twenty-five years. She lives on a ranch in the heart of rodeo country (southern Arizona). Some evenings, she wanders over to watch her neighbors in friendly roping competitions. A western restaurant in town offers weekly bull riding and mutton busting. But Rachel much prefers a quiet ride on her gentle paint horse, Lady.

curiousabout
BREAKAWAY ROPING
BY RACHEL GRACK
AMICUS LEARNING

What are you